What's Next?

2012 EDITION

A Look Over the Next Hill for Innovative Churches and Their Leaders

Dave Travis

Leadership ✖ Network

ISBN 978-0-9853402-0-9
Second Printing

Leadership ✳ Network

This book is published by Leadership Network. For more information about
Leadership Network, see www.leadnet.org

To order multiple copies at great prices please send an email to
dave.travis@leadnet.org

Single and Kindle versions are available at Amazon.com.

Contents

The Big Picture

INTRODUCTION

Predictions are a perilous business; the future is endlessly elusive, inevitably surprising.

Peter Drucker, Leadership Network's grand mentor, understood this. He chose to focus on what he called "the futurity of present events." The better we understand what's happening, the more likely we are to anticipate what's next.

In these pages we'll take Drucker's approach. The idea is to trace the outlines of the recent past and attempt to discern the contours of the future.

For anyone who has been paying attention, these past two decades suggest disruptive trends in any number of areas. Once church life evolved; now it transforms. Again and again, old wineskins burst in the interaction of church, technology, and social revolution. When we are caught in the crossfire of change, and are forced to adapt, we seem to be at our best.

We see that happening at this very moment. Innovations and new solutions continue to emerge at a rapidly accelerating pace. Our client churches, out front on all things made new, define the themes for the next season of ministry. Some ideas may be recognizable; others will surprise and intrigue us, all the more as we analyze the futurity of present events.

Consider the pages to be a wide mural, rendered in bold colors and broad brush strokes.

Our goal in this report is to render a consistent picture, a credible futurescape, and to anticipate the kind of wild cards that defy context.

Consider the pages to be a wide mural, rendered in bold colors and broad brush strokes—the body of Christ at large. Each congregation paints its own little patch of the canvas, but the backdrop is one we share and define together.

That background, in turn, interlocks with the even greater picture created by the culture of the world—sometimes in colors that complement, sometimes in glaring challenge.

This, of course, is the same as it ever was: the dialogue of church and culture across time. But we live in particularly revolutionary days. We hear the voice of God commissioning us as ambassadors to a rapidly materializing future. Only God is unchanging; the world moves along, the church takes new forms, and, not incidentally, we ourselves become new people.

Our prayer is for the grace and wisdom to transform the days ahead, even as we are transformed, striving together until the kingdom may come and his will may be done.

A WORD ABOUT YOU

This report has been prepared for you, Leadership Network's key clients. For more than fifteen years, we've studied the world around us. We've done our own research, as well as reviewing the best work of others, to better understand our cultural climate. We've reflected upon the data and drawn conclusions, in the hope of helping to shape the future of our clients and their ministries. In this report, you'll find a great many of those insights.

To paraphrase Mark Twain, we believe the rumors of the church's death have been greatly exaggerated. In every generation we've heard the end of the Christian church proclaimed. But we believe the future for innovative and larger congregations is bright indeed—particularly when compared to other churches and movements in the U. S., Canada, and Europe.

Church leaders, especially evangelicals, tend to see the glass half empty. Cultural change is frightening; it forever appears to us that we're losing our channels to the next generation. Statistics are brandished in panic, showing Christian influence melting away as rapidly as the polar ice cap, and everyone bemoans the onset of a new dark age of secularism.

Yet it seemed this way a century ago, even two centuries ago. Somehow the work of God goes on. It navigates the changes, lives to fight another day, even gets out front in places. Isn't that work, after twenty centuries, worthy of our confidence?

Negative stories about megachurches or evangelicals hit the newswire with regularity. Twitter, the blogosphere, and other social media amplify the issue until it appears to be a catastrophe of epic proportions. There is hand-wringing, navel-gazing, weeping, wailing, and the gnashing of teeth. And we are our own worst critics. If something happens at a particularly visible church, then we jump to the conclusion that it represents an epidemic. We generalize too much.

Here we think Leadership Network provides a crucial reality check. Our research and experience base covers a global movement. We aren't on the outside of the churches in question, looking in—we have staff serving and worshiping in them each week. Their insight is a bit more substantial than hit-and-run journalism.

Last year alone, we held fifty-five small gatherings of leaders, with six to a dozen or more churches represented at each gathering. Our directors talk every day with lead pastors and strategic church team members, and they come away with accurate frontline insights.

We certainly aren't pumping artificial sunshine on a gloomy day. We don't ignore the problems, crises, and obstacles that churches are facing, nor do we assure comfortable ministry happily ever after. We do believe that the Christian faith in the Western world is alive and well, and that the vital signs are robust and vigorous.

But you make the call. We offer in this report the trends and insights to help you evaluate the evidence, then decide whether you share our general optimism about the future of ministry. We predict you'll be encouraged to move ahead with confidence; that even as troubling issues rear their heads, new openings for the gospel emerge as a direct result. For thoughtful and well prepared leaders, there will never be a shortage of fresh opportunity.

Again, we believe in keeping an ear to the ground. In a world of movement superstars, bestselling authors, and lead conference speakers, our true heroes are among the hundreds of pastors who are celebrities only in their communities and circles of influence. These are the men and women who fight on the true front

These are the men and women who fight on the true front lines of the battle. They tend to establish roots, systems, teams, plans, and local networks that establish multigenerational change for the better in their communities.

lines of the battle. They tend to establish roots, systems, teams, plans, and local networks that establish multigenerational change for the better in their communities. They may never be the media's "flavor of the week," but they play the long game, and make the changes that endure.

At Leadership Network, we're betting on just this group of ministers, because we've tracked their ministry. We see the changes they've made and the fruit they've borne. It is to their work that we're dedicated, finding every way possible to help them carry out the age-old work of the gospel in fresh new ways.

Our vision is to help them preach, teach, disciple, and baptize more people who, in turn, will go out themselves in exponentially increasing numbers to be salt and light in a dark and thirsty time.

Our Leadership Network programs help them to do better the things that Jesus did while on earth. We help them heal, feed, clothe, tend to the mentally ill and disabled, to minister to prisoners; and to recover, restore and renew our culture.

Our direct programs serve a relatively small handful of leaders who in turn influence other churches to do likewise. In this way we focus our investments of time and energy to yield the most impact we can.

WHY WE FOCUS ON INNOVATION

When the world changes, innovation becomes necessary. Innovation, in turn, changes the world.

Our focus is not on every new idea, but on those few that transform the shape of future ministry.

We don't pursue innovation for its own sake. Its value is in creating a higher level of performance. One field might have any number of innovations, all of them representing stronger performance. Our focus is not on every new idea, but on those few that transform the shape of future ministry.

We value innovative entrepreneurs because they are game-changers. They create movements of ideas and actions that galvanize those around them. When the forest begins to seem too thick, they are the ones who invent new tools for path-clearing. These innovators work within their own cultural milieu, making the gospel come to life within the specifics of how local people live and think.

Everett M. Rogers' classic study *The Diffusion of Innovations* (Free Press, 2003) offers some instructive ideas—for example, the concept that larger organizations are better equipped to start and spread innovations to a wider field.

But what about the edges? Some would insist that innovation happens at the edges and works its way in. It's the rebels, the upstarts on the fringes, who come forward to redefine the field for others—or so goes that version of how things work.

We can point to younger, smaller churches who enjoy the freedom to change things, and who often seed new ideas and innovations into the Christian ecosystem. They may even grow to become the "larger organizations"; or the existing larger organizations co-opt their ideas while those on the edge move on to something new.

But pushing an idea across the broad expanse, from an obscure starting point, is a challenge. There is a need for "opinion leaders" to get on board. It's more likely to happen with larger churches with greater resources. They're in better position to try something new without sacrificing their core strengths.

There's a fine line here. The unchanging church will become tired and stale if it fails to keep up with the times and the trends. It's true not just for churches, but for any kind of organization.

At Leadership Network we give special attention to innovation. We set out to help the entrepreneurial change agents refine their ideas into solid plans, then drive them to impact. In addition, we are the "diffusers of innovation," as Rogers would have it. We share with others what those teams are learning, so new ideas can be adapted to other places and other local contexts.

What about theological foundations? Some readers will look for a doctrinal justification for each observation. These are always valid questions, of course, but this report is designed to be concise and factual.

Other organizations actively pursue those debates, which fall outside our set purposes.

THE WAY WE WERE: REVISITING 2000

Let's take two steps back before taking steps forward. What are the changes we've observed over the last dozen years?

- **In 2000 there were fewer megachurches and innovative churches.** Let's feel good about the fact that we've seen a wave of church startups and, yes, growth in established churches. See item 1 in the **Foresight** section for specifics.

- **In 2000 there were more "big box stores."** We saw the explosion and ensuing decline of the all-purpose, big box category-killer at one location. There was a fear that small churches, too, would go the way of Mom and Pop shops. Compare the decline of the enclosed mall experience. These models endure, but Internet-enabled sales have left their mark on the retail universe. Item 4 will describe how that relates to churches.

- **Multisite churches were hard to find.** After looking high and low, we found 128 of them in North America in 2001. Now there are at least 3,000. See Item 2 in the **Foresight** section for more on this trend.

- **The Externally Focused Church trend was in its infancy.** These are churches giving special attention to serving "the least of these" in their communities—again, a very positive sign. For larger churches, local mission has moved from afterthought to essential—seen as an authenticating mark of a vigorous church. See Item 6.

- **A phone was just a phone**. If you carried a Blackberry, which handled e-mail and contacts, you were truly elite. The smart phone was a matter of science fiction; the iPhone wasn't seen until 2007. Cell phones are now at the center of personal communication of every kind, including in ministry. See Item 11 in **Foresight**.

- **AOL and Yahoo were dominant Internet companies.** E-mail addresses still tended to reflect public companies rather than private servers. Thus pastors are now reached at their churches' dot-coms rather than @aol.com. "Walled garden" Internet services such as AOL have totally given way to the Internet's open frontier. Church websites were curiosities, and people weren't sure what to do with them.

- **"High speed Internet" was for the privileged**. Now, as streaming HD video is commonplace, even smartphones are transmitting data at broadband speeds.

- **Music meant compact discs.** The first iPod wasn't released until late 2001. The minister's old "cassette ministry" has given way to podcasting and streaming worship services—giving any church a potential international reach.

- **Pine and Gilmore's *The Experience Economy* (1999) was all the rage.** The authors spoke at several Leadership Network events. The book's language has become part of the tapestry of churches whose "Experience Pastors" come up with creative ways to connect.

- **No Facebook, Twitter, or YouTube.** The term "blog" wasn't used until 1999, and most existing "weblogs" were one-way soapboxes, rather than encouraging interaction. The explosion of social media has changed the way leaders connect with the public in a busy world. See Item 12.

- **The economy was more fluid.** Though the Dot-Com bubble burst in March, 2000, but even with a mini-recession, the economy clicked along and financing was less of an issue. See the next session for the "new normal."

Context

THE INVISIBLE BOND

"Blest be the tie that binds"—including the loose cooperation of different groups working toward the common good. Sociologists call it *social capital.* People, relationships, money, time, effort, causes, and resources connect people who, for example, want to see safer streets or better care for the homeless.

These networks, seldom noticed, lie beneath what we consider to be civil society, and they're held together by the glue of shared vision and values.

We believe that large churches are the most effective and efficient bundlers of social capital in a community.

We believe that **large churches are the most effective and efficient bundlers of social capital in a community.** These churches are the best equipped to mobilize large groups of people to use their time, talent, and treasure for purposes that make the neighborhoods better places to live. Yet they're equally effective in achieving such goals across the world.

Consider a typical nonprofit, or even a local business organization. Its ability to expend social capital pales in comparison to what can be done by any of several large churches in the same community.

Social media, as it becomes more common among church leaders, only widens the gap. Using Twitter, e-mail blasts, or Facebook posts, these congregations are beginning to extend their mobilization abilities.

Why are we making this point? Social capital presents critical opportunities to maximize God's common grace in a community and engage outsiders in activities that are good not only in themselves, but as powerful, positive reflections on the church. In a time of increasing hostility toward organized religion, the world watches ever more closely to see what the church will do for its community.

We believe larger churches have been the unsung heroes of their communities for decades; that is, their social capital has been undervalued.

But does size matter? Smaller congregations can make their mark, of course, but there is an undeniable power in numbers. A large church can provide the free work force to clean up the park after a July Fourth parade, for instance. It can offer its worship center for a town meeting or high school graduation. There are things only the larger congregation can do on a scale that captures the community's attention.

And even more commonly now, larger churches have the capacity to partner with public schools, government agencies and local non profit groups to release waves of volunteer and financial capacity in joint projects.

THE GLOBAL FACTOR

Leadership Network finds its focus in the spiritual scene of North America and Europe. But we're well aware of what God is doing across the globe.

Through the history of Christianity, we've seen how worship and ministry have taken forms appropriate to all varieties of culture. The gospel never changes, but its story can be told in every dialect. It's intriguing to observe the most effective churches in other societies. In a third world environment, the work of the church will appear strikingly different than in suburban American Christianity, but one hope, one faith, one baptism is still manifest.

We want to underline the point that we celebrate the diversity of worship expression in many cultures, because we're reminded of the greatness of our God.

Conversely, other cultures have lessons to teach us. A Chinese or Chilean ministry is free of the tradition-bound assumptions that drive us; they have a way of getting to the root of the gospel and showing us some element of worship we're missing, some strategy for evangelism we'd never have hit upon, due to our "cultural blinders."

Many times we've sent missionaries to take the gospel to remote areas. They've come back bearing new ideas that have added freshness to our worship and service. This is a global synchronicity that surely pleases God's Spirit.

On the other hand, we feel it's unwise to go as far as to assume, in the light of Eastern approaches, that Western approaches must be less biblical. Ultimately the real question doesn't arise from style but from substance. Are people experiencing Christ? Are they being liberated from the power of sin? Are they using their spiritual gifts?

It's not necessary to reflexively grab every new idea, any more than it's necessary to impose old ideas in new places. We love the variety of expression; our focus is simply on organized, gathered churches in type and style.

At the same time, we recognize that many leaders around the world are eager to learn from Western churches, including the newer trends we're implementing. They come from every corner of the world to see for themselves, and to consider how they use what they're seeing. Meanwhile, the U. S., Canada, and Europe provide crucial funding to add new layers of effective ministry in those more distant places.

As we all know, the globe is shrinking. No longer is any country an island, complete unto itself. Economies interlock; ministries and missions interlock. This can be an advantage, because it means more mutuality and improvement in all sectors.

IT'S THE ECONOMY, OR IS IT?

The recession has left its mark everywhere—on our friends, our families, our cities, our churches. Leadership Network clients have not been immune, but we believe the damage has been greater elsewhere. We've heard the reports of foreclosure, layoffs, and other cutbacks.

In fact, the global financial crisis presents a ready scapegoat for failures of every kind. If a market segment struggles, blame the economy; if a church stumbles, same explanation. The truth is often a bit more complex. Looking a bit deeper into a specific situation, we might find church division, moral failure, or simply bad leadership decisions as the root issue. To our knowledge, we have no clients in foreclosure trouble.

Unfinished construction—churches as well as condo units—has been a sign of the times. We've heard of churches suspending building programs due to the lender's inability to fulfill commitments made to the church. Those driving by would assume the church was struggling, but it might well have been the bankers, who have, in fact, been hit the hardest during this recession.

Most of our clients seemed to reach the bottom of the trough in 2009, with conditions steadily improving since then. A board member explained it this way: "Seven fat years, followed by seven lean years." Looking back, he would appear to have it right, as we all enjoyed the go-go economy of 2002-2008, and the recession may end up matching it in length.

For this reason, we take the role of Joseph and caution our clients to get their storehouses in order. Financial prudence is more critical than ever.

With the recession driving prices down, greater opportunities present themselves in the areas of land, buildings, or mission opportunities.

We've seen a trend toward budgeting spending at eighty to ninety percent of the previous year's income. Overages are then reserved as "opportunity funds" for strategic purposes throughout the year. With the recession driving prices down, greater opportunities present themselves in the areas of land, buildings, or mission opportunities—a classic example of turning stumbling blocks into stepping stones.

Other churches and leaders have been wise enough to take a greater role in helping church attendees reduce debt. For several years, there was a nationwide de-leveraging in which savings rates among the population were rising and debt was falling. Church attendees could then give more in spite of reduced incomes. Late 2011 saw a slight uptick in debt ratios, but the emphasis on debt reduction and frugal living has played out in evangelical churches, particularly larger ones.

Yes, we've walked through the valley of the shadow of debt. But we've seen many of our clients make the right adjustments to weather the storm, and come out even stronger.

ALL CONTEXT IS LOCAL

Our job is to see the forest for the trees. We get the lay of the whole land, and summarize the movements of innovative and larger churches as a whole. The goal, of course, is to project the health and growth of the forest in the changing seasons. We measure against the past and then envision the future.

A church may have multiple sites, even dozens of sites. Each site is set within a community all its own. Each community is unique. Larger churches, we define, have the best understanding of how this works. They are careful to adapt to micro-contexts and cultures, rather than laying down a prefabricated plan that never varies.

As a matter of fact, this is true all around the world. Wherever churches are growing, they are responding to and adapting to the distinct attributes of the soil in which they're planted.

Leadership Network has client churches in every kind of community, at every economic level, with every racial identity; in dense urban areas, suburbs, and exurbs.

THE YOUNG GUNS

If past decades offer a clue, we can expect to see the advent of ten new "hot young gun" pastors in the next ten years. They'll start churches with explosive growth, and subsequently show up on the platforms of various conferences. Everyone will take a good look at these new gurus of church growth, hoping to extract a seed idea or two.

Yet the new breed will develop ideas that rise from foundations laid over the past thirty years. The key will be that these leaders will be gifted at reaching the younger generations. Therefore they'll be celebrated.

This isn't a prediction—it's the classic script of passing time.

Old conference notebooks reveal to us that many of the 2002 thought leaders are no longer at the center of our ecosystem. Yet they built the steps to this year's platform.

Foresight: The More-Ofs

Our Foresight section begins with a list of the things we expect to see *more of*—with a *why-so* or two to consider.

1. **More Megachurches.** The megachurches will outlive us all.

     We define them as any protestant church averaging two thousand or more in weekend worship, including adults and children. Once there were a handful; now there are almost too many to count, indeed, more with each passing census.

     The stereotypical media story focuses our attention on the older churches that have declined, or on the spectacular downfall of a leader. What they fail to cover is the tsunami of newer churches, as well as the latest members of the 2,000-Plus Club.

     Wherever the population booms, churches grow and thrive. It's a basic missiological principle that holds true everywhere in the world. In the simplest terms, rapidly growing communities are the most likely to host rapidly growing churches. New housing growth translates to new church plants and established churches that have been "reinvented."

Another factor is mobility. Americans are more mobile than Canadians, far more mobile than Europeans. For any of a number of reasons, Americans move multiple times in a typical lifetime. The ebb and flow of residents in a community mean that an area can have stagnant growth numbers, but still have thriving churches. New neighbors mean new prospects.

Our next item offers further support for the growth of larger churches.

2. **More Multisite Churches and Campuses.** One of the more striking trends of the previous decade has been the emergence of the multi-location church as a normal condition. Currently at least fifty percent of megachurches are also multisite churches.

Even so, the multi-location church isn't strictly a phenomenon of the megachurch. We've observed multisite churches with as few as four hundred regular attenders.

As a rule, this strategy has boosted growth beyond the standard limitations of a single site. Growing churches are adding sites to reach new people in various ways.

About fifteen years ago, a consultant was talking to the leader of a large and growing church that was relocating. This church had recently purchased 132 acres of land on a busy thoroughfare. "It won't be big enough," warned the consultant.

Given the pastor's particular vision, the consultant may have been right. But the plum site of the past, with flat space and excellent access, is no longer so easy to find—a moot point, given the possibilities of multiple campuses.

The multisite movement has opened up a great deal of diversity in the kind of space that can now serve as a worship center. It has also enabled the churches to be very strategic about micro-targeting demographic areas. A site can be opened in a bedroom community with young families—or in the inner city, with a mission-targeted ministry.

As America becomes more diverse, specific people groups can be reached at devoted sites. There's also the opportunity to develop systems for leadership development and other infrastructure, which only accelerates the growth potential.

We don't expect that multisite movement to let up anytime soon.

We don't expect that multisite movement to let up anytime soon. In fact, these churches are constantly reinventing themselves, working on new solutions as challenges arises. Even in Europe and elsewhere, as evangelical churches grow, we're seeing multiple locations as a viable strategy.

3. More Internet Campuses or Ministries. A few years ago, I listened in as two prominent lead pastors of growing churches debated a point of contention. Each man had planted lots of churches and campuses. What they disagreed about was the meaning of the term *Internet campus.*

For one, the phrase described a natural extension of multisite ministry; for the other, the whole idea was a glaring oxymoron at best, a new heresy at worst. But as the discussion ensued, he conceded the possibility of having an extensive Internet ministry, complete with worship, small groups, and other functions. It was doable; it was, in fact, happening. "Just don't call it a church," the skeptical pastor concluded.

We understand his distinction and value his perspective. But in the end, it's all the same to those who participate in the online experience. A decade from now, an Internet campus will be the new normal, complete with a campus pastor and a full team commissioned to nurture, disciple, and counsel the participants.

> A decade from now, an Internet campus be the new normal, complete with a campus pastor and a full team commissioned to nurture, disciple, and counsel the participants.

There will still be churches who consider the Internet as a gateway only, a way to leverage technology to invite "lurkers" to put in an eventual physical appearance—in essence, the heir to television ministry in past eras.

But others will embrace cyberspace as a legitimate mission field of its own; "virtual" souls will simply mean souls. God's redemptive Spirit will draw people to himself there, just as he has done in sanctuaries or family life centers.

We'll continue this conversation in Item 11.

4.   More Closed Big Box Stores; More Closed Churches. We repeat: Big box churches are enjoying robust health.

For retail stores, there's a different reality.

We expect to see new churches moving into closed, expansive retail stores, as well as reopened church buildings enjoying second lives with new congregations.

The wave of 1990s-era retail store closings should continue. It's a well-documented business story that much shopping has moved from brick-and-mortar to mouse-and-modem. We've seen CompUSA, Borders, and Circuit City shut down multiple locations, often seeking refuge as Internet retailers themselves—if you can't beat 'em, join 'em. Amazon.com is one of the biggest winners, allowing customers to price-check whatever they see in a physical store, then match the price online. One-click shopping, combined with two-day delivery and customer reviews, is a formidable challenge to traditional retailing.

Walmart, Target, and other smart entities will hold onto their niches, but few new names will enter those markets. Home repair and improvement warehouses, and other stores allowing customers to test or to touch before buying, will survive. But the Internet exodus will continue. This can be a serendipitous moment for new churches looking for non-traditional spaces.

Commercial areas may soon be begging churches to move in, if for no other reason than to keep the properties from decline and blight from setting in.

The question is whether the developers and owners will want churches as tenants. Municipalities have fought the incursion of storefront churches for a decade, fearing loss of tax income and constant weekday consumer traffic. But economic crisis can change the game. Commercial areas may soon be begging churches to move in, if for no other reason than to keep the properties from decline and blight from setting in.

Another development: closings and mergers among small to midsize churches. A struggling church can survive as a new location of a multisite church. In fact, growing multisite churches are gaining the opportunity to be more selective as offers increasingly come their way. Cost-free or inexpensive properties will open up.

We counsel caution in the decision to assume a property. An opportunity may seem to fall from heaven today, a better one, or several better ones, may be available tomorrow. We're not discouraging our clients from taking on new locations—just advising them not to rush headlong into what may prove to be a lesser option.

Jesus said that when a man builds a tower, he should first count the cost. Corollary: when a church moves into a big box retail space, it should think first about the expenses of retrofitting. They're considerable.

But so are the advantages: higher visibility locations with plenty of parking. This will be a trend to watch.

5. More "Second and Third Tier" Cities. The old conventional wisdom was to look for large, innovative churches in the biggest cities and their suburbs. This has also changed in the last decade or so.

Expansive church campuses are cropping up in all types of locales. A few could be classified as rural or even as villages; predominantly, we see them in towns, exurbs, and resort/retirement havens. The large church movement transcends the metropolitan community.

As a matter of fact, many communities host a cluster of larger, innovative churches, each one representing a slightly different theological stream or primary worship style characteristic. There will be movement among the crowds between these churches, but that's true of churches everywhere.

It would seem that, as people become acclimated to large churches and their resources, they find it more difficult to move to a relatively small church.

Later this year, Leadership Network will offer a report addressing the "where" question for the future.

Again, it's often suggested that megachurches and larger churches will phase out because "no one is moving to the suburbs anymore; they're reclaiming the cities and rejecting sprawling church campuses."

There are various reasons why those pundits have it wrong.

First, it's true that some middle class residents have migrated back to urban areas. The other side of that coin is that suburban growth has continued to overmatch that trend. The exurbs, the ring of cities beyond the suburbs, have also continued to grow. Many of our clients are finding them to be fertile fields for new churches, new sites, and remade churches.

Secondly there are the polls of millennials, who indicate a strong preference to enter the suburbs once they start families—thus following the patterns of the past seventy years. It's become the case not only in North America but in Europe as well.

Like Elijah, we look at "these old bones," our cities, and wonder if they can live again. They can, particularly with churches smartly built to reach younger seekers. But the greatest movement and opportunity will continue to be moving in outward circles from those cities.

Authenticators

The previous section listed the *more-ofs* we expect to see during the next few years, as churches strategize to increase their impact on the world around them.

Now let's explore the expansion of *social capital bundling*. During the past decade, we've seen this factor grow from seed form to a current blossoming among larger, more innovative churches. As churches carry out various practical ministries that improve their communities, these ministries—in our view—become the "authenticators" of the church locally. The church has credibility not because of the pastor's communication abilities, but because the members act for the good of the surrounding area.

Younger people in particular are no longer won over by Christian apologetics or social programming. They believe the church is validated by how it collectively lives out its core beliefs. This isn't to say that it's the case for every new church visitor, but social capital is a strong ingredient in the recipe of churches that are reaching people currently.

6.   Community Serving. This term describes the bundle of activities that help to define how a church is *for* its community. These activities include ways in which a church is engaging

Community serving defines how a church is for its community.

"the least of these" in the area. In our Leadership Network shop, we have described these strategies with two of our leadership communities.

- Our **Externally Focused Church** community highlighted the ways in which churches developed strategies to better serve their communities, as well as mobilize and disciple their congregations at a higher level.

- Our **Missional Renaissance** community extended those ways to forming networks and practical coalitions with other community partners in coordinated ways—often with the church, or churches, as capstone partner.

These actions are perfect examples of larger, more innovative churches bundling human, financial, and influence capital to serve their communities effectively. Not only do these strategies have a powerful impact on their communities, but they are highly effective in impacting the church's participants themselves to a deeper walk with Christ. Thus we have a win/win for church and community.

Local initiatives such as these bring us to our seventh item.

7. Globally Connected. Like the church itself, missions continually find new forms and outlets as the world changes. Missions and missionaries reinvent themselves. The latest wave has been stimulated by cheap communication and travel, as well as by forward-thinking parachurch groups who have partnered creatively with larger churches.

Some younger adults feel that a church is not authentic without a visible global outreach program to connect with at a heart level.

Larger, more innovative churches want to feel a sense of ownership and a deep connection in global projects. They find ways to engage in that arena. It could be an outgrowth of local community outreach to a people group residing in the local community. Or it could be the natural extension of the mission experiences in other countries that helps participants rethink their local community outreach.

Some younger adults feel that a church is not authentic without a visible global outreach program to connect with at a heart level. It's not an American but a global phenomenon. The developed world is not alone in pursuing globetrotting mission engagements.

More than ever before, the latest generation grasps that its nation is no island, but a citizen of the world at large. If it's happening in their business, they expect it to happen with their church.

Our next item shares these global implications.

8. Church Starting and Planting. It seemed like a radical move a decade ago, when Leadership Network formed a core group of churches to aggressively train, support, and launch at least four new churches each, per year. But the trend only accelerated.

Nearly every large church is now involved in planting new fellowships at some level. Churches are engaged in startups, either from their own church programs, or from a network program composed of two or more partners. As a result, this past decade has been a time of aggressive growth in terms of new churches. In fact, we documented a few years ago that church starts were now exceeding closures—a significant trend reversal.

In fact, we documented a few years ago that church starts were now exceeding closures.

In Europe, we see churches following suit, planting all across the continent and not just within their own respective countries.

Again, the planting factor is an authenticator. Younger generations expect the church, if it has credibility, to be reproducing itself. So we see the larger church starting up a new plant several neighborhoods away. Or it could be a "franchise," with similar worship style and values, in another state. Then there are those who are opening churches in other countries.

Will the trend continue? We notice a significant ramping up of support organizations to assist in church starts and plants. More than 4,500 leaders gathered for one church-planting conference. Even several old-line denominations have renewed their efforts in starting new churches.

In Europe, the trend has been toward the "missional community" approach to planting—an approach that is now making inroads in the

U.S. and Canada. We'll address this experience in a later report, along with the "organic church experience" and how it relates to our context of planting. We simply lack the space for such a detailed subject here.

Pay careful attention to missionaries coming to the U. S. Canada, and European countries from places like Central America, Asia, and Africa. Missions are now a fully two-way street. These church starts are on the increase. They begin by attracting people groups corresponding to the countries sponsoring the plants. It's just as it was one hundred years ago, when many European-based churches were started in the U. S. and Canada. But over time, the distinctions begin to blur through intermarriage and aggressive outreach—which again leads us to our next item.

9. Racial and Ethnic Diversity. Younger generations have come of age with diversity as an expected condition. They see no reason why the church would not "look like America" as they see it. Thus racial and ethnic diversity become another authenticator of a genuine church. If they look around and see a homogeneous congregation, they tend to discount the effectiveness of the church experience.

Since 2000, our surveys have pointed to larger churches having a fairly high degree of racial diversity, as compared to smaller churches. Another factor here is that larger churches are more likely to reflect social diversity among staff members. This has been an issue we've observed on our surveys of Anglo leaders for some time, but we are beginning to see Anglo churches become more aggressive in creating a more ethnically diverse church.

A few caveats:

- This may be a more active issue among Anglo-oriented churches; less so among African American, Caribbean, Central American, and African immigrant churches. This isn't to say these churches lack diversity—just that the leaders perceive it as less of an issue.

- Diverse communities in the U.S., Canada, and Europe are not evenly distributed. In some regions of the countries, there is a higher degree of racial diversity than in others. The issue becomes an authenticator when the minority groups exceed a ten to fifteen percent ratio.

- Some potential members, who would represent a minority in a given locale, will naturally seek out a church that welcomes diversity. But this number is not as large as one may suspect.

If you are a large, growing, innovative church in a diverse community, your participants, staff and leadership will reflect that reality or risk being discounted by younger generations.

Nevertheless, this is a rather new rule: If you are a large, growing, innovative church in a diverse community, your participants, staff and leadership will reflect that reality or risk being discounted by younger generations.

Prepare for controversy with our next item.

10. Transparency. Here is the issue: Do church leaders make decisions and handle money "in the light of day," or do things happen behind closed doors?

The degree to which this is an issue can vary, but it will increase in importance as an authenticator—not only for prospective members, but for the community at large and its local government.

Once upon a time, church members simply trusted their leaders. Some still do. But in the world we now inhabit, trust depends to some extent upon reasonable transparency. In the future, it could become a critical issue.

Trust depends to some extent upon reasonable transparency.

U. S. churches exist in a legal gray area. They are required to follow not-for-profit regulations in many areas, without being required to file reports and returns in the way other not-for-profit organizations do. They must follow rules on political activity, compensation, insider dealings and the like, but they are still given considerable leeway in the matter of financial reporting.

Even when denominations require their churches to file reports, the results may not be shared outside denominational offices.

Going forward, we feel that voluntary transparency will bolster churches in the eyes of the public—members and outsiders alike. Younger adults will insist upon it, being accustomed to detailed reports from other charitable organizations.

Areas of impact:

- **Annual Reports.** Already, churches are more often posting annual activity and financial reports on their websites. These show members and others the progress of recent months, but also demonstrate financial integrity.

- **Audited Financial Statements.** The churches we serve tend to get financial audits when they are approaching a financial institution for financing. We believe large churches should invite annual audits by qualified firms, or at least every other year, alternating with management control checks. The entire system of stewardship gains credibility when funding is shown to be above board.

- **990 Filings.** Very few U.S. churches file an IRS 990 Not for Profit return. I don't believe they should be required to do so. Having said that, I also believe larger churches should prepare this form every year and release it without filing it with the government. Again, this is a confidence builder inside and outside your church. We also suspect there will be a move in the future by the IRS to require this form to be filed by churches that exceed a certain threshold of income. Now is the time to prepare for that possibility.

- **Compensation Opinions and Policies.** Wise larger churches are using surveys and consultants to inform their compensation agreements with staff. It's a good idea.

These aren't the favorite topics for most church leaders we know. Their lives and ministries have enough challenges without the added layers of expense and tough questions that invite criticism. Even so, we believe that openness and transparency should be hallmarks of any authentic church. Practically speaking, these things help win confidence from the community. In the long run, they're worth the headaches. We suggest the items above to demonstrate to the world that our churches are beyond reproach.

More money questions will be raised in Item 15.

The Obvious

This section deals with trends that parallel the culture at large—corporate and economic trends that you should be quick to recognize.

11. "Web-Enabled" and the App World. Church websites are no longer cute afterthoughts. Larger and innovative churches grasp their centrality in the modern world.

Our clients pay careful attention to their web presence. They understand how a website represents the "zero moment of truth" experience, the first impression that counts most strongly. Google scientists coined the above phrase when they discovered that today's customers no longer wait for the "first moment of truth"—physically inspecting a product—to make an emotional evaluation.

The "zero moment," before that, comes when a prospective member searches for your church in a web browser. In other words, before the scrupulously friendly Welcome Center, before the all-important parking experience, people will inspect how a church presents itself in cyberspace.

But the web offers more than a virtual handshake and a PR presentation. Many churches are using it to link congregants to other resources: Bible studies, sermons, online classes. In the future, we'll see even more varied uses of the Internet.

The web offers more than a virtual handshake and a PR presentation.

Most of our clients are now benefiting from online giving arrangements. We've already discussed the phenomena of Internet campus of ministry. The interesting development has been the church getting ahead of the curve for once, quicker in mission-related purposes to use the web than other social institutions have been. The trend will continue as new tools develop.

Experts are looking to the rise of the app interface—smaller applications that work from smart phones to become a ready tool for the church member. At present, most of these tend to be stripped-down versions of mobile websites, organized to perform a handful of purposes well. Surely apps are part of the ministry future, but we're watching to see exactly what creative uses will be found.

In the meantime, Item 12 is already upon us.

12. Social Media. It's now difficult to remember that Facebook was once for the kids and Twitter seemed like a useless update of what your friends ate for breakfast.

No one jokes about social media anymore. A decade ago, blogs from a few tech-friendly leaders were bringing ongoing conversations here and there. But Facebook and Twitter have created an entirely new way of connecting people.

Some have tried to create "walled gardens," protected web places for connecting participants. We believe those will wither in the face of the dominant social media players. Leaders use these tools to enhance their bonds with people in the community. Younger people, as usual, take this development for granted as genuine relationship.

We can bemoan it all as "superficial"; we can advocate the need for deeper connections. But smart phones are leading the conversation. Their saturation with social media is redefining the way we people reach out and touch each other. Congregations and leaders who celebrate, encourage, and participate in this environment will reap rewards.

There are other opportunities opened by social media. Larger, innovative churches tend to grow through word-of-mouth endorsement, participant to potential

Social media means that even the shy crowd can tell others about your church.

participant. Social media means that even the shy crowd can tell others about your church.

Forward-thinking churches are finding new ways to announce initiatives, ask for help, or send encouragement through these applications. We can't say whether Facebook or Twitter will endure, a decade or two onward; they are new wineskins that came in to replace the ragged ones, and they, too, will wear thin at some point. For now, they're important containers for the gospel we seek to share.

13. Interns and Residents. Where will all the staff come from in the future? Most likely a combination of places, as always. But one of the key development arenas will be structured intern and residency programs, targeting younger generations who come forward to ask for practical training.

This trend mirrors what is going on in other corporations. Not-for-profits and other institutions are mobilizing interns for a variety of tasks. Additionally, a growing number of high schools are requiring low level experiences that are often called internships.

> The internship has somewhat replaced the part-time job as a combination résumé builder and experience base.

The internship has somewhat replaced the part-time job as a combination résumé builder and experience base to pad school entrance and corporate job applications.

Churches have had internships for some years. What's new is seeing them as strategic for development of new staff and Kingdom workers for other contexts. We've seen the same development with "pastoral residents programs," that act as finishing schools with longer time commitments and stipends.

Our larger, innovative clients are upgrading these programs so that they do more for both parties. Otherwise they'd struggle to compete for the highest level of talents among interns and normal staff. Full-time team members become acclimated to strong intern programs, finding their own productivity increasing—not to mention the rewards of the hand-up to the next generation of Kingdom workers.

It doesn't always go according to script, of course. Either side can have a poor experience. Intern programs need to be carefully organized, closely monitored.

Leadership development remains a critical issue. Our clients are excited about developing a range of customized leadership development programs at all levels, knowing they're offering a gift to the future of ministry.

14. Outsourcing. This subject would fit nicely with the item that follows it. But we want to give it specific focus, because we look for a parallel with developments in similar-sized not-for-profits and small companies—namely, a wave of functions being outsourced on an "as needed" basis. These are tasks and ministries that, in the past, would have been the responsibilities of staff and key volunteers.

A discussion among a executive pastors, several years ago, brought this to my attention. One of them asked, "How much are the rest of you spending on financial administration between personnel, software, and other costs?"

There were various answers. Some said they were turning to a combination of volunteers or part-time staff; others were looking to full-time staff as always, or, in certain cases, software licenses. But one participant said, "I'm confused. We pay a service to handle all these things for us. We just pay them month-to-month on an agreed upon annual basis."

He showed that his church was saving money, decreasing headaches, and raising the service level.

We see more churches following this leader's direction, not just in accounting but in other areas. Staff is freed up to emphasize their particular gifts and special goals. It's all made possibly largely because so much of our work has now entered the digital domain, and because people in general are now more readily accessible through modern communications. Information is more readily accessible.

We have envisioned several other kernels of outsourcing that we feel will only accelerate.

15. Discipleship in Generosity. Here's what we were hearing so often from pastors in 2000: "I never mention money in my sermons. It turns people off."

This thought trend turned out to be a very unfortunate one for many churches.

In spite of the recession, the U. S., Canada, and Europe still enjoy high incomes and comfortable lifestyles as compared to the rest of the world. Finance is never far from the minds of most people in these nations. A consumer society attends to its method of consuming.

They grasp that spiritual growth comes in the grace of giving.

Churches are emerging from the old state of denial, and launching programs, sermon series, and small groups that approach financial issues from many angles. And apparently, people aren't being "turned off." When the subject is intelligently approached, people respond in the desire to know God's perspective on a matter of such urgency. They grasp that spiritual growth comes in the grace of giving. Then, of course, the attention to finance pays off in church members becoming better stewards of their income and their giving.

We've discussed authenticating marks. This matter might well fit into that category, except that it has become so common as to be almost taken for granted. The wider culture pays more attention to the value of thrift, and of bringing expenditures into alignment with one's values. Why wouldn't we in the church have something to say?

16. Capital Campaigns—Without a Building. Again, churches are keeping pace with the nonprofit world. A fund-raising campaign need not be about a new building.

The first wave was the setting aside of some fundraising, in the midst of a building campaign, for designation to a specific mission project.

The second wave was setting aside an amount to fund the staff of such a project—as well as the new facility.

The current wave has moved beyond architecture. It focuses on "ministry and mission expansion."

Speculations

In our final section, we take a stab at the futurity of the present events we've detailed. These would apply to a few churches and would constitute "mini-movements" at best. Yet each could represent sparks that could grow into fires.

17. The Retro or Vintage Wave. For every broad movement, somewhere we find a reactive one—perhaps a backlash of sorts.

For example, we run across a few churches or venues who are intentionally using simple, acoustic music and a more traditional style—and reaching lots of people.

We've also heard several reports from younger churches in stylish areas. Every six to eight weeks, they invite a choir or a gospel choir to lead worship. "Whenever we announce the choir is coming," they say, "we blow it out in attendance." It's the pause that refreshes.

As one of our favorite pastors says, it's not an age thing; it's a mindset thing.

It's worth remembering that vintage movements tend to emerge during down economic cycles.

We look for something similar in church architecture. Today a church can look like almost anything—which is good theology. But expect buildings with a traditional feel outside and inside, while retaining modern technological infrastructure.

18. Bonds and other Finance Vehicles. Church bonds have been around for many decades. Most of the time, they proved to be a reliable system of financing construction-type projects. Occasionally, a prominent scandal or failure would decrease enthusiasm for them.

Bond financing also tends to rise when banks set tight conditions and higher interest rates. For the first part of the last decade, credit availability was widespread. But things have changed.

With interest rates so low for fixed income investors, there is rising enthusiasm for churches to get back into the bond markets for building projects. Some of that will actually be driven by church members that are willing to finance the construction project in this way, in exchange for a fixed return higher than they are earning on other investments.

19. LLC Special Purpose Companies for Asset Holding. I've heard of churches with members who urged their congregations to purchase property and even build facilities to lease over a certain time frame. They would form a for-profit LLC toward that end, with lease payments reimbursing investors over time.

As with Item 18, these investors seek a premium return compared to government securities, and to help their churches.

Such situations pose risks for both parties. Good legal and tax counsel would be absolutely critical before considering them. But undeniably attractive possibilities will present themselves to churches willing to move quickly on certain properties that can be acquired at depressed prices.

20. Measuring Impact. Part of our mission is to help our clients move from ideas to implementation to impact. We do this through our Leadership Community and Innovation Lab processes, where ideas are refined into implementation plans, and progress is then measured.

That measurement is essential, encouraging our clients to keep working toward their initial goals. We've helped churches discover standards of measurement in mission-related areas.

One client provides a perfect illustration of that. This client had obtained permission from city hall to occupy and rehabilitate a site as a worship center. In the city, that decision was a controversial one.

The church made a strong commitment to serve the whole city as creatively as possible. But how to measure its success? Members began to keep track of hours devoted each week by its members, in service through other community organizations and externally focused small groups.

They multiplied total hours by the dollar figure offered in the independent sector for volunteer work. Now they were able to discuss their value to the community in terms of an accepted standard of financial value. Then they told the congregation that number and celebrated it in church and among community leaders. This created allies and apologists for the church's presence—often in unlikely places.

Some churches are holding high the standard of providing so much value that if the church were to vanish, the community would mourn its absence.

Some churches are holding high the standard of providing so much value that if the church were to vanish, the community would mourn its absence.

Larger, innovative churches have grown adept at telling their impact stories in moving ways. Anecdotal evidence can be powerful, but key metrics are equally essential. Outsiders and non-believers in particular want to see the numbers—and within the church, younger members will use those numbers as authenticators of genuine Christian mission.

Large church visibility is a two-edged sword. Some in the community will respond positively, see the church as a beacon of hope. But hard-liners will inevitably see the church as a target for derision. They'll be even more vigilant in finding faults, real or imagined.

In general, churches need to do a better job of measuring their impact and telling their stories, to those within and those without.

Wildcards

Here are a handful of unlikely events. Perhaps none of these things happen, but each of them could be possible, creating positive or negative waves that leaders would have to address. No one anticipated the fall of the World Trade Center, the world financial crisis, or the advent of social media. Expect none of these specifically—but expect the unexpected in some form.

- **Outages: Cell phone network or Internet domain.** From time to time, we've seen shutdowns of wireless networks. Users are naturally very impatient with the sudden disruption to so many portions of their daily routine. Outage = outrage. The fact is, smart phones have become one more dependence in the modern world. We do our banking, we check our stocks, we get our news from them. Imagine an outage in Internet routing and trunk lines, disrupting those churches that rely on these tools for communication or service delivery.

It may not sound too threatening now, but we're surely entering a new era of cyber-terrorism and cyber-war. Those with axes to grind can attack specific sites or even an entire network within a region. At Christmas 2011, a think tank was attacked by "Anonymous" to steal credit card information simply for harassment purposes.

- **Revised tax laws: charitable donations minimized.** The entire not-for-profit world watches anxiously, having seen it come close to fulfillment in 2011. The largest givers would see the largest impact. Our belief: Churches would come out the least scathed among nonprofits, because they have frequent and intimate interaction with those who support them. Even so, such a development would send huge ripples within our world.

- **More facilities off limits to churches: NYC school ban spreads.** In December 2011, the U. S. Supreme Court allowed a circuit court ruling to stand, starting the process of excluding churches from using schools for weekend worship in New York City. Another NYC agency has followed suit, extending the church ban to other kinds of public spaces. A precedent has been set—will it become a trend? At the height of the church planting movement, we could conceivably see thousands of congregations put out in the cold. The Supreme Court may be forced to re-confront this issue.

- **Economy back with a vengeance: Recovery picks up speed.** A dramatic turnaround could spill over to other regions. It's worth noting that the Canadian economy, for one example, has suffered much less than the U. S.; yet certain other regions have fared poorer. The U.S. could become a relative safe haven for investment again from around the world.

This increase, along with normal government efforts to pump up employment in an election year, could see some short term financial improvement. An uptick in the U. S. housing market would signal a stronger economy, with higher waters lifting other boats. It could also mean inflationary pressures on staff, facilities, and other costs.

- **Billy Graham, the Sequel:** Who will be the next great evangelist with a worldwide impact? I've predicted for years that we're likely to see a native of India or some other Asian country, fluent in English, who can appeal to the West. He or she would have a simple lifestyle and approach, offering content both basic and advanced.

We'd expect such a leader to be male, more than likely, and to use modern technology without being driven by TV and radio. It's easy to envision him (or her) being the subject of thousands of independent websites set up by followers with *samizdat* (bootleg-type) recordings of the leader's messages, in a more popular—and less orchestrated, prefabricated, or merchandised—movement. Such an event would change the paradigm of leadership in large churches.

- **War**. It's the perennial wildcard. No one could have been expecting a prolonged war in Afghanistan, or a "war against terror" that changed our way of even defining war. We can agree that our troop withdrawals represent a positive note, but it also means certain losses to industry—and increases of hundreds of thousands in the numbers of people seeking jobs. Some of the economic recovery will be blunted by this factor.

Meanwhile, the nature of warfare continues to evolve, as we read news stories describing remote aircraft and other advances that lessen the need for ground troops.

What about another war, perhaps with Iran or North Korea? The re-escalation of world tensions, redeployment of U. S. NATO, and other forces will come at massive cost, but human and financial. We would expect spiraling government budgets leading to even greater levels of debt and tax. Churches, like every other part of society, would feel the effects.

Conclusion

After nearly thirty years of service, our question remains the same: How can we be useful to you?

At Leadership Network, we identify innovative, entrepreneurial churches to engage with our core processes. We call these forums Leadership Communities and Innovation Labs. We share what our clients are learning through our global online conferences and informational resources.

While our clients pay fees for various processes and services, we are primarily funded by visionary and generous donors. Our initial launch came on U. S. soil, but we now serve client churches in Canada and Europe, and we plan to expand even further.

Our "elite" processes are limited to selected clients, but we're always eager to build new relationships and to find out how to serve new friends—from Ideas to Implementation to Impact.

Let us hear from you.

About the Author

Dave Travis is the Chief Executive Officer/Chief Encouragement Officer of Leadership Network, a nonprofit organization focused on helping **Innovative Entrepreneurs in churches move from Ideas to Implementation to Impact.**

He has worked with senior leadership teams of large churches in the U.S., Canada, and now Europe, since joining Leadership Network in 1995. In a typical year he will personally speak to over two hundred leaders of these churches on a confidential basis.

He is a graduate of Georgia Tech and The Southern Baptist Theological Seminary. He and his family live near Atlanta, Georgia.

The opinions expressed in this work are those of the author. They are informed by insights from a variety of team members at Leadership Network, as well as trusted key clients. Leadership Network prides itself on its openness to differing perspectives in a complex world.

The team at Leadership Network is composed of over twenty professionals who actively serve churches through programs ranging from Leadership Communities, Innovation Labs, Global Online Leadership Conferences, books, and digital tools.

Feel free to add your own thoughts and opinions by e-mailing the author directly at dave.travis@leadnet.org. Or follow him on twitter @ davetravis. To see regular email updates on matters in this booklet email dave.travis@leadnet.org with "email updates" in the subject line.

Dave also wants to thank Rob Suggs for his help with this project.

About Leadership Network

Leadership Network assists Kingdom Entrepreneurs to move from Ideas to Implementation to Impact. It does this primarily by working with strategic church leadership teams in the U.S., Canada and Europe.

Our Strategy:

EXPLORING CONVERSATIONS

- Discovering leaders of influence and innovation
- Listening to their Strengths, Opportunities and Challenges
- Being curious about future possibilities
- Exploring Trends that will impact the wider kingdom
- Finding Innovations that lead to higher performance

"Let's Talk Together"

We believe that meaningful conversations can change the world.

ESTABLISHING CONNECTIONS

- Connecting the "dots" of data and conversations to reveal a larger trend
- Seeing the bigger kingdom vision beyond ourselves
- Connecting leaders to one another for deeper conversations

"Have you connected with this idea or person?"

We believe that by connecting leaders we catalyze Kingdom change.

EMPOWERING COLLABORATION

- Ideating for Kingdom impact to help leaders imagine and map future possibilities
- Challenging to action leading to improved performance
- Encouraging accountabilities to peers for encouragement and refinement

"Let's work together on this"

We believe that collaborative environments of peers lead to better ideas and results.

ENCOURAGING MULTIPLICATION

- Affirming and blessing leaders for their kingdom impact
- Informing the Church by sharing what we and our clients have learned
- Inspiring others through the stories of God at work among our leaders.
- Surfacing new conversations that we need to explore

"Let's build on this or Let's multiply this"

What's Next at Leadership Network

Leaders are always focused on what's next. What is God doing now? How can we join? What is the "Aha" to help us move further?

Leadership Network is here to help you and your staff move from ideas to implementation to impact!

LIFE STAGE LEADERSHIP COMMUNITIES

For Senior Pastors Only! Leadership Network's Life Stage Leadership Community groups consists of a relational peer network of senior or lead pastors that share similar ministry challenges and that desire connections to others serving in similar ministry career stages.

Next Generation Pastors (serving churches in North America)

Designed for senior pastors age 25-45, leading a church of 800+ attendance and experience serving in the lead pastor role for at least 3+ years. These pastors are life-long learners desiring mentoring from more seasoned senior pastors as they work through leadership challenges in the early stages of their ministry careers. This two-year experience includes 4 meetings consisting of coaching by mentor pastors, peer learning in small groups, personal leadership plans and relational connections that last a lifetime.

For more information contact linda.stanley@leadnet.org

Senior Pastor 2

The Senior Pastor 2 Leadership Community is designed for senior pastors age 45+, leading a church of 2500+ attendance and experience serving in the lead pastor role for at least 10+ years. These pastors are simultaneously building and strengthening their senior level leadership teams, their churches, and their local and global communities.

For more information contact wayne.smith@leadnet.org

INNOVATIVE PRACTICE LEADERSHIP COMMUNITIES

Leadership Communities are a proven process to help church leader teams achieve twice the results in half the time. Peer groups of 10-12 teams are formed to help dream, create and execute ideas into real action and tangible results.

Rapid Growth

The Rapid Growth Leadership Community helps churches set bold goals for future growth and assist them in developing solutions for the inherent challenges and opportunities that come with rapid growth.

For more information contact tim.nations@leadnet.org

Global Connections

What is your global missions ministry doing differently today in view of our changing world than it was doing ten years ago...or 30 years ago? If your church is thinking about improving your global missions initiatives, we invite you to join missional leaders from 8-10 other churches for this two year journey that is designed to transform your church's impact on the world.

For more information contact eric.swanson@leadnet.org

Leadership Development

Leadership Development is the #1 issue leaders mention when we ask them to list their most urgent ministry challenges. In a collaborative learning environment with other large churches, you'll take an in-depth look at new ways of replicating, multiplying and developing leaders.

For more information contact brent.dolfo@leadnet.org

Generous Churches (EUROPE)

Designed to address the increasing need to build a culture of generosity in churches throughout Europe, Leadership Network is partnering with Stewardship (UK), Crown Europe, Christians Against Poverty (CAP), and the Lausanne Committee, to facilitate the European Generous Churches Leadership Community. Accelerate your efforts to develop a "culture of generosity" in your church through a series of highly specialized, interactive gatherings, enhanced by relationships with fellow pace-setting churches.

For more information contact nicola.james@leadnet.org

Marriage Ministry Leadership Community

Today, perhaps more than ever, the church needs to have a comprehensive strategy for supporting the marriages in the church and community. This leadership community will expose your team to the best and most effective models of marriage ministry in the church today and will challenge you to create a plan that will be effective in your unique church environment.

For more information contact chris.willard@leadnet.org

Multiethnic Churches

If your ministry leadership team, your governing board and your church body share a passion to transform "the most racially segregated Sunday hour" to one that reflects the multiethnic diversity of our changing world, then join us on this two-year journey. Learn with like-minded peers that are blazing the trail for other churches to follow.

For more information contact linda.stanley@leadnet.org

Churches with Non-Profit / Charity Organizations

In our ever-changing and increasingly challenging economy, churches are often looking for ways to serve their communities through various not-for-profit ventures. This community is designed for churches that have already launched a 501(c)(3) venture and are wanting to learn from others and collaborate in helping each other maximize their efforts and effectiveness.

For more information contact wayne.smith@leadnet.org

INNOVATIONLABS

InnovationLabs are 12 month experiences that will bring fresh and new ideas to areas that have grown old and tired or jumpstart your team in a new ministry area. Beyond typical brainstorming, your team will be stretched to think beyond the boundaries of current reality to answer the question, "What's around the next corner?"

Multisite Artist Development

If you are a full-time worship arts director or pastor in a multisite church, with oversight of the weekend experience, worship and creative arts, Leadership Network is bringing together innovative church leaders and creative professionals to help you develop a comprehensive worship arts development model for your church.

For more information contact tim.nations@leadnet.org

Multisite JumpStart

This unique InnovationLab is designed for church teams planning your first multisite location(s) and will focus on the practical how-to's of location, leadership and structure. You will have the opportunity to be exposed to some leading multisite practitioners and consultants as well as other churches that are on the multisite launch pad, and you will walk out of the room with an action plan for launching your first campus.

For more information contact wayne.smith@leadnet.org

Generosity Ministry

The Generosity Ministry InnovationLab is focused on helping churches create a culture of generosity and stewardship. This InnovationLab will feature the results based collaboration Leadership Network is known for and will help your team shape a plan to create a culture of giving and stewardship in your church.

For more information contact chris.willard@leadnet.org

Justice Ministry

Ministries of mercy deal with the symptoms of people's brokenness. Ministries of justice traffic in the systems that create those symptoms. In this InnovationLab you will explore the big issues facing our world today and what your church can do to engage some of the big systemic problems facing the world today.

For more information contact eric.swanson@leadnet.org

Social Media and Communications

The digital landscape is now dominated by social media and with the growing majority interaction now taking place on mobile devices. Through this medium, churches have an unprecedented opportunity to be in conversation with members, guests, and potential attenders. The Social Media and Communication InnovationLab is designed to help innovative churches develop a ministry strategy that will impact newcomer and member engagement through various social media channels.

For more information contact tim.nations@leadnet.org

Internships

There is a shift from viewing Interns as "free, or low-cost workers" doing ministry menial tasks to asking the question, "How can we expand the Kingdom both in and through our interns?" Participation in this InnovationLab will help your team analyze and utilize their resources in equipping and strengthening the Interns and Internship Program in your church.

For more information contact wayne.smith@leadnet.org

For a complete and up to date listing

of all our program offerings, visit

http://leadnet.org/whatsnext

Additional Resources

EMAIL AND WEB

Leadership Network publishes a regular, free e-newsletter featuring the best in church innovation. Just go to www.leadnet.org and hit the subscribe button at the top of the page.

We also carry over 100 downloadable papers, podcasts and other free resources. Go to www.leadnet.org and look under the resources tab.

And each week we post new information via our blog to serve church leaders.

BOOKS AND LEADIA

See our latest books here: http://leadnet.org/resources/books - we have over 60 to choose from and you can order right in our online bookstore at http://100x.christianbook.com

Leadia is the name of our new iPad friendly multimedia, interactive tool that helps you learn from some of the best leaders. http://leadia.tv/Leadia/

UPCOMING LEADERSHIP COMMUNITIES AND INNOVATION-LABS AND OTHER PROGRAMS

Leadership Network offers these peer driven experiences that help church teams move from ideas to implementation to impact in a variety of areas. These experiences are application only but to inquire see this page. http://leadnet.org/whatsnext

In addition we offer a few open gatherings each year.

GLOBAL ONLINE CONFERENCES

Watch our blog and e-newsletters for our online conferences you can attend from your office or home. These three times a year experiences enable you and your team to hear and interact with great leaders around the world.